New Boy

John and Marilyn Talbot

Illustrated by Rhiannon Powell

Contents

Chapter 1

The Move

The car pulled into Wellington Square and stopped outside number twelve.
'This is it, Danny,' said his mum.
'This is our new home.'
Danny looked up at the house and he didn't like it.

They went inside.
'This will be your room, Danny,' said his dad.
Danny looked around the empty room, and thought, 'My old bedroom was much better than this.'

A few days later Danny was shown around his new school by Mr Belter.
'Well, Danny, this is your new school, we hope you're going to like it here,' he said.
But Danny was thinking 'My old school was much better than this.'
Mr Belter said to the class 'This is the new boy, Danny Lock, and we hope he's going to be very happy here.'
Danny looked at the children in the class and he knew he wasn't going to be happy.

Back home, Danny's mum and dad were talking.
'Danny's not happy here,' said his mum.
'I know,' said his dad, 'But it takes time to settle into a new home and a new school.'

A few weeks later as Danny's mum was putting clean sheets on his bed, something fell down. It was Danny's notebook. It lay open on the floor. Danny's mum picked it up and looked at it. She got a shock.

Chapter 2

Note Book

Danny's mum knew that he didn't like his new home, but she had no idea just how much Danny hated Wellington Square and everyone in it.

Danny had drawn cartoons of everyone and written unkind things about them.

Crazy Mr Keeping keeps snakes everywhere,
in his house, in his hat-
and even in his hair
steady on Bruce old boy!
What's got two heads,
ginger hair and silly grins?
-Tony and Tessa, the 'Potty twins'!
apple for you sir!...
Her name is Jamila,
if you haven't met her yet...
She makes you sick - she's the teacher's pet!

Rocky and Max are stupid names!
Together they play stupid games!
SLOW DOWN ROCKY!
Help
What I would like to do to Waterloo School.....
BOOM!
Before
Then..
After!

Danny's parents were very upset to find out how unhappy Danny was.
'What can we do?' asked his mum.
'Let's show it to his teacher,' said his dad.
'He might know what to do.'

Mr Belter flicked through Danny's notebook.
At first he thought the cartoons were quite funny,
until he came to the one of himself.
Then he stopped laughing.

‘Danny must be very unhappy,’ said Mr Belter.
‘What should we do?’ asked Mr Lock.
‘We need to make him feel more welcome here,’ said Mr Belter. ‘So I will talk to the class, if you will talk to Danny.’
Mr and Mrs Lock agreed.

Chapter 3

Make Friends

The next day Mr Belter talked to the class while Danny was out.

'So we have all got to try harder to make Danny feel welcome here.'

The class said they would try.

That evening Danny's mum talked to her son.
'You have got to try and make friends,' she said.
'OK,' said Danny, 'I'll try.'

Over the next few days Jamila, Ben, Rocky, Tony and Tessa tried to make friends with Danny. Even Kevin tried!

But trying didn't work.

'Do you want a go on my Game Master?' said Kevin.

'Why would I want to play on that old thing when I have this,' said Danny and he pulled a brand new Game Master 2 out of his pocket.

On his way home Danny was talking on his mobile to one of his old friends.
'I hate this school. The kids here are boring.'

Just then a gang of older boys ran up to Danny and snatched his mobile.
One boy called Spike pushed Danny so hard he fell and hit his head on the wall.
Another boy grabbed Danny's Game Master 2 as it fell out of his pocket.

The boys ran off leaving Danny on the ground holding his head.
He couldn't help it, he began to cry.
Then he saw Kevin coming around the corner.

At first Kevin was glad to see Danny crying,
but then he felt sorry for him.
'Who did this?' he asked as he helped Danny up.
'I don't know,' said Danny, 'but one of them was called Spike.'
'It's the Cobble Road gang,' said Kevin.
'They come around here sometimes.'

Kevin walked with Danny to his house and carried his bag for him.

'They took my mobile phone and my Game Master 2. I hate living here,' said Danny.

'So do I, sometimes,' said Kevin.

Chapter 4

No Fuss

Mrs Lock was very upset when she saw her son.
But Danny didn't want his mum to make a fuss or call the police.
She cleaned the cut on his head and put a plaster on it.
Mrs Lock was glad Danny had a friend at last.

The boys went upstairs to Danny's room to play computer games.
Kevin was much better than Danny who never ever got past level three.
Later Danny went down to get a snack.
When he came back upstairs he heard Kevin laughing.

Kevin was reading his notebook.
'You shouldn't be reading that!' said Danny and he tried to snatch it out of Kevin's hand.
But Kevin pulled it away and kept reading.
'This is so funny,' he said.

Then Kevin opened the page with him on it.

Kevin stopped laughing.

There was going to be a fight.
'So you think I've only got a small brain, do you?' said Kevin.
'Well… I did,' said Danny. 'But now… I don't.'

'So what size is my brain now?' yelled Kevin, coming towards him.

'Big,' said Danny, 'very... big.'

'How big?'

'You've got the biggest brain in Wellington Square,' shouted Danny.

Mrs Lock heard the shouting and ran upstairs.

Mrs Lock burst into the room expecting trouble. Instead she found the boys laughing their heads off. Kevin was only joking, he really wasn't angry at all.
'You boys alright? asked Mrs Lock.
'Yeah, fine,' said Danny. 'Just fine.'

Chapter 5

New Friends

The boys got on very well after that.
Kevin talked Danny into helping out with the school play.
Danny was good at art so he painted the sets.
He also started to make friends with the other kids in the play.

A few weeks later Mrs Lock was cleaning Danny's room and she picked up his notebook. Danny had done more drawings and written some new things.

'I hated Wellington Square when I first came here but now it's OK.
Kevin is my best mate and some of the others aren't so bad.
But that Mrs Valentine...

But that Mrs. Valentine....
V1
...She's totally off her rocker!!